TERSUR ITYOKOSO

BEFORE THE VOWS

PATHWAY TO A GODLY AND LASTING RELATIONSHIP

BEFORE THE VOWS
PATHWAY TO A GODLY AND LASTING RELATIONSHIP

To order copies of this book,

Book layout: **Iorwuese Mtomga**

Cover design

Published by
Lumfater Multimedia
Makurdi, Nigeria
lumfater@gmail.com
0703-865-7585

DEDICATION

Dedicated to my Father,

Rev. T. T Ityokoso

You set me on the right path in life and relationships and you continue to a be great source of inspiration to me

CONTENTS

ACKNOWLEDGMENTS

◇◇◇

MY LOVE AND GRATITUDE TO my adorable wife - Gift; my lover and best friend. Our friendship started like a joke in Gboko at an NKST Mission Retreat conference and grew into courtship and then marriage. Thank you for providing the enabling environment for us to keep learning from each other and growing. Your partnership with me in this marriage journey so far and in our work with young people has been a great source of inspiration, strength and fulfilment. This book would not have been possible without you by my side; you are simply the best.

Also to my three wonderful kids; Esther, David and Davina. You guys are wonderful father trainers and have made fatherhood a pleasure.

My deep gratitude to my parents and particularly my Dad, Rev. T. T. Ityokoso. Your commitment to providing true guidance and a godly example for me in life and in relating with the opposite sex has been a great anchor in my relationship life. I still remember that fateful day when you brought out several little books to our room for us to choose from and read, from which I found a book on opposite-sex relationships and took to reading it. That was my first contact with a relationship book, but the insights I got from that book coupled with your careful instructions on the subject set me on the right path in relating with the opposite sex right from my primary school days into my adult life. Your God-inspired guidance and careful instructions have brought me this far in life and marriage. Thank you for your continuous support in my marriage and for being a great source of strength, inspiration and encouragement.

I remember with great gratitude the Rev. Albert Strydhorst, who offered guidance and direction to me in my years of struggle with relationships with the opposite sex and in trying to make a choice of a life partner. You followed up my relationship with Gift from its inception to our marriage and you administered the vows we exchanged on our wedding day. Your wife Carolyn held my wife close and gave her all the support she needed before, during and after our wedding. Your discipleship of us among other young people at NKST Anglo Jos, helped greatly in stabilizing my Christian faith and guiding me to acquire the right family values. I will forever remember with fondness your interactions with me during your time of stay in Nigeria. May the good Lord continue to bless and keep you.

My profound gratitude to Rev. Prof Tersur Aben, my pastor, who has always been a great father to me and my wife. Your words of encouragement to us before our wedding and your message on our wedding as well as your regular messages on the pulpit in church continue to inspire me towards godly living. Your fatherly role to me has extended to giving me job opportunities and granting me unfettered access to you. Thank you for being a true father to us.

Thank you very specially, Mr David Tyokighir, for the time you took in your busy schedule to take us through a pre-marriage counselling course. Those sessions were very illuminating and really helped to prepare us for marriage.

Great Thanks to Dr Paul and Mrs Jossie Ubwa, for being a strong pillar of support to us before our marriage and over the years. We are blessed to have you in our lives and we look forward to continuing to enjoy the parental support and encouragement that you continue to give to us.

My deep gratitude to Paul Humbe, the Director of Fine Pearls Youth Ministries. Thank you for your interest in me since after my secondary school education. You have continued to be of great encouragement to my spiritual life. Thank you for all you do to encourage my family and all my Christian ministry endeavours. May God's grace continue to abound for you in your tireless work on the lives of young people.

Big thanks to Mr Fater Mtomga, my big brother and friend. Our relationship started right from secondary school as father and son and has grown over the years. I still remember the time you took during my courtship with my wife to guide us through resolving a serious issue that came up. Since then, God has continued to use you on different occasions to encourage me. I really do appreciate you, sir.

I am very grateful to Rev. The Shepherd Loho-U-Ter Shadrach, who has been a source of great inspiration since we met through Fine Pearls Ministries. I had the opportunity to work under him directly in Jos and since then he has been a great source of encouragement to me in my Christian life, ministry outreaches and marriage as well as my book writing efforts.

My very special gratitude to Dr Torese Agena, who has been a great source of inspiration to me through his humility, his love and commitment to God and the great work he and his wife do at Priscilla and Aquila Centre for Peace. Despite his very busy schedules he took time, within a very short notice, to read through every page of this book's manuscript and made very fundamental inputs that brought about certain additions to this book that led to an improved depth on the subject addressed by this book. Sir, I am most grateful for your great support and encouragement.

A special thank you too to Rev. Prof. E. O. Usue. Thank you for taking time out of your very tight schedule to go through this book and make a review. I am very honoured and deeply appreciate your encouragement.

My special appreciation to my dear friends who have helped me in doing a lot of thinking, putting the final touches and planning towards the publishing and launch of this book. Doofan Shambe, Deborah Asooso, Solomon Awua and Nahandoo Ichoron, you did me a great honour by giving your time to this project. Your inputs here and there added great value to this book. I will forever be grateful for the sacrifices you all made to see that this book came out well. May the good Lord reward you in a thousand folds.

My profound gratitude to the editors of this book, my big brother and friend, Daniel Itiza Akaahan, and my dear friend of many years, Nahandoo Ichoron. You two are a true blessing to me. Your commitment to editing this book was a great encouragement to me. Your critical analysis, remarks and corrections were immensely valuable and have contributed greatly to this book's quality. I almost ran away from Nahandoo because of how thorough he went about editing this book, from pointing out mistakes to disagreeing with some views and my presentations to outrightly re-writing certain paragraphs. But I stuck with him through long calls and arguments that led to very exciting decisions about this book's content. I lack the right words to appreciate you. May God remember your labour of love and reward you abundantly.

I am very grateful to Iorwuese Mtomga for undertaking to do the layout design of this book and have done an excellent job at it. Thanks a lot, brother.

Finally, time and space will not allow me to talk about; Arc. Barns Ekpo, Arc. Grace Akanni, Arc. Asema Agelaga, Arc. Mimi Gerna, Aondofa Usur, Naregh Agelaga, and a host of others; my dear friends with whom I had discussions at one point or the other about relationships with the opposite sex. Please bear with me if I've failed to acknowledge you more directly. I really appreciate you and pray the Good Lord to bless you immensely and prosper you all.

May God's countless blessings be on you all, in Jesus' name.

FOREWORD

◇◇

THE BOOK IN YOUR HANDS comes from a successful family man, who has helped younger people stay faithful in their singleness and get ready for fulfilling marriages. Many books have doubtlessly been written about singleness, preparing to, and actually getting married. Written by Christian authors, such books sometimes are scriptural expositions on the subject of marriage – and there is a place for that. The practical how-to questions are not always answered though. That's where this book is different.

I first met Tersur Ityokoso in the early 1990s as a secondary school student, which I was too. He was God-fearing and has remained consistent in his faith all through the years. So, at the risk of sounding rather old, I have literally seen him grow into a professional and a Christian family man, who is passionate about the success of the marriage institution. With his wife beside him, Tersur has demonstrated this passion through the regular *Singles' Hangout* events they have held for several years now. Their stated aim is to "help youths to maximize single-hood and prepare for marriage". Like all things Christian and good, this venture has not been without its challenges, but with God on their side, this couple have weathered the storms of opposition and forged ahead with the call of God on their lives. My wife and I have also been privileged to visit and speak at the *Singles' Hangout*.

The author has worked with singles and writes scripturally and from years of practically helping young people through what could be difficult years and one of the most consequential and life-shaping decisions anyone could make – marriage. This book is a practical guide on how to make this decision. The author doesn't shy away from discussing the difficult issues but takes the reader by the hand and walks them through. There may be questions that you may have found it difficult to ask, probably out of conservatism, this book doesn't shy away from those difficult questions – it raises and answers them.

I have been privileged to work on this book and trust me, it is a very useful resource. I hope that you'll find the insights herein rewarding and recommend this to someone else to get helped as well.

Daniel Itiza Akaahan
Teacher, Writer and Editor.
Makurdi, Nigeria.

PART 1

NECESSARY PREPARATIONS

CHAPTER ONE

WHAT'S YOUR PLAN

THE CONCEPT OF TIMES AND seasons has been stressed throughout the pages of scripture. Right from creation, the Bible tells us that God Himself set aside times and seasons such that in Gen. 8:22, God says: "As long as the earth remains, there will be springtime and harvest, cold and heat, winter and summer, day and night". Every young person needs to understand that this concept of times and seasons is also true for our lives and we must take our lives seriously enough to diligently seek God's wisdom in understanding the times and seasons of our lives.

> **It is not possible to achieve success without first dedicating some deliberate efforts to planning**

The wise King Solomon speaking about time said: "There is a right time for everything" (Eccl. 3:1). Every young person who wants to live a fulfilled life on this side of eternity must take those words seriously and be curious to know the right time for every aspect or phase of their life. Seeking God's direction and guidance on when to take certain steps in your life is one very fundamental issue you must have to sort out very early in life. I am referring to a point in your life when you have gained clarity of purpose and of how God will have you take specific steps concerning important aspects of your future.

As you make the decision about what career to pursue and are on the path to the desired career, the next major decision should be about when you will be ready to start taking deliberate steps concerning a life partner. Making that decision will help you focus on other important things while you wait for that time to come. It will save you from distractions and unnecessary waste of time and energy. That is what happens when you have a plan.

Planning is a very important and necessary aspect of success. It is not possible to achieve success without first dedicating some deliberate efforts to planning; that is why it is often said "he who fails to plan, plans to fail". our path towards marriage should necessarily be planned out and properly thought through. It should never be left to chance or luck. You should plan it out starting with when you will begin to take deliberate steps towards starting a relationship.

You will also find that when you save and conserve your time and energy through such planning, your set time translates to a goal which though you may not be actively working on, subconsciously there is some work going on towards such a goal. When that set time comes, you will be amazed at the ease with which things will take shape and pull together.

The kind of plan for when to start a relationship, as I am advocating doesn't have to be figured out by you all yourself. It will be wise to seek guidance about it to be sure the plan you come up with is practical and realistic. And that guidance must not follow another person's exact pattern, but as you seek to ascertain what will work for you, it will be wise to hear from more than one person. The Bible says it clearly that "in the multitude of counsellors there is safety" (Prov. 11:14b). From their counsel

> **...but as you seek to ascertain what will work for you, it will be wise to hear from more than one person.**

it will be clear what agrees with your unique circumstances and peculiarities.

Most importantly, this kind of plan must be undertaken under God's clear guidance. It should come from your understanding of God's will for your life and a conviction in your spirit that it is time to take a step towards a serious relationship at a particular point in time. Such a conviction should be followed with careful and relevant preparations towards its actualisation.

CHAPTER TWO

HAVE SOMETHING TO OFFER

ONE IMPORTANT PREPARATION YOU WILL have to make before facing the issue of a romantic relationship is to spend time developing yourself. This is one thing that won't come naturally.

You have no business thinking of any serious relationship with the opposite sex until you have something meaningful to contribute to another person's life. That meaningful thing can only come from years of developing one's self. Such contribution should be in at least three areas- emotionally, spiritually and mentally. This is important because as you form close attachments with someone else you are going to have certain influences on each other knowingly or unknowingly. So if you are not well equipped to give something positive and tangible then, you will offer something negative that may ultimately wreck that person's life.

The words, ***"As iron sharpens iron, so one man sharpens another,"*** found in Proverbs 27:17 seem to leave the task of "sharpening" a man in the hands of the other people we relate with. And I believe one won't be wrong to say that if the relationship between two people is not going to sharpen them then it will certainly blunt them. Put differently, if a relationship between two people is not going to make them better it will certainly make them worse.

Secondly, that verse is also reminding us of something a good number of youths seem not to appreciate: the fact that relationships have responsibilities and obligations, and one major responsibility is to 'sharpen' the other person. So, unless you intend to fail the other person, you will spend time to equip yourself adequately to live up to that responsibility. This is the basis on which I say wait until you are at a point where you have developed yourself sufficiently for that responsibility before you

> **Relationships have responsibilities and obligations, and one major responsibility is to 'sharpen' the other person.**

step in. When you master yourself and can resolve certain important issues about your personality, you will be better positioned to contribute meaningfully to someone else's life.

Wait until you are at a point where you have developed yourself sufficiently for that responsibility before you step in.

There is also a dire need for you to develop your relationship with God. One of the ways to do this is to learn to hear from God. This is one aspect of yourself that I am so sure if you develop, you will be at your best in making the right choices and doing the right things because you are clear about His leading and guidance in your life.

This too is one aspect that you will need very seriously before any other thing about the relationship takes any serious turn. Because if you cannot hear God well enough you are bound to follow your human wisdom which has failed many and will certainly fail you.

The issue of hearing God is so fundamental that I will conclude this chapter by sharing an abridged version of what Nicky Gumbel has written on the topic in his book *"Questions of Life"*. He says: "God guides us in various ways. Sometimes God speaks through one of the ways discussed below; sometimes it is a combination. If it is a major decision He may speak through all of them. They are sometimes called the five "C.Ss."

1. Commanding Scripture

God still speaks today through the scripture to guide our step and help us understand His will. He may speak to us as we read. The Psalmist says, "your statutes... are my counsellors" (Psalm 119:24). That is not to say we find God's will by opening the Bible anywhere at random and seeing what it says. Rather, as we develop the habit of regular, methodical Bible study we begin to find it quite extraordinary how appropriate each day's reading seems to be for a particular circumstance in which we find ourselves.

Sometimes a verse seems almost to leap off of the page at us and we sense God speaking through it. It helps to make notes when we study God's word, because you might only find a connection of several of God's instructions after to review what He told you some time back. Without noting it down it might be impossible to remember not to talk of making a connection to what he has said to you some time back.

> **God still speaks today through the scripture to guide our step and help us understand His will.**

2. Compelling Spirit

The way God guides us is very personal. When we become Christians the Spirit of God comes to live within us. When He does so, He begins to communicate with us. We need to learn to hear His voice. Jesus said that His sheep (His followers) would recognize His voice (John 10:4,5). The more we get to know Jesus, the easier we will find it to recognize His voice.

The following are three examples of the way in which God speaks by His Spirit;

i.   Often God speaks to us when we pray

We must always remember that prayer is supposed to be a two-way conversation. If whenever we pray we only speak to God and never take time to listen, we make a serious mistake and are denying ourselves of an opportunity to hear God's voice. God's guidance may come during prayer by way of a thought just coming into our minds; people sometimes describe it as "impressions" or feeling it "in their bones."

> **The more we get to know Jesus, the easier we will find it to recognize His voice.**

Obviously such thoughts and feelings need to be tested (1John 4:1). Is it in line with the

> **If whenever we pray we only speak to God and never take time to listen, we make a serious mistake and are denying ourselves of an opportunity to hear God's voice.**

Bible? Does it promote love? If it does not, it cannot come from a God who is love (1 John 4:16). Is it strengthening, encouraging, and comforting (1 Corinthians 14:3)? When we have made the decision, do we know God's peace (Colossians 3:15)?

ii. God sometimes speaks to us by giving us a strong desire to do something

"God ... works in you to will and to act according to His good purpose" (Philippians 2:13). As we surrender our wills to God, He works in us and often changes our desires. This is one reason we must never dread finding out God's will. Because contrary to what some people might believe, God's will often is revealed with the appropriate desire or urge (or grace) to follow it through.

iii. God sometimes guides us in more unusual ways

The Bible has many examples of God guiding individuals in dramatic ways. He spoke to Samuel as a small boy in a way in which he could hear with his physical ears (1 Samuel 3:4 – 14). He guided Abraham (Genesis 18), Joseph (Matthew 2:19), and Peter (Acts 12:7) through angels. He often spoke through prophets both in the old and new testament (for instance, Agabus in Acts 11:27, 28; 21:10,11). He guided through visions (sometimes referred to today as "pictures") as well as through dreams (Matthew 1:20; 2:12; 13, 22).

3. Common Sense

When we become Christians we are not called to abandon common sense. The psalmist warns: "Do not be like the horse or the mule, which have no understanding but must be controlled by bit and bridle or they will not come to you" (Psalm 32:9). The New Testament writers often encourage us to think and never discourage us from using our minds (for instance; 2 Timothy 2:7). If we abandon common sense, then we get ourselves into absurd situations.

It is true that God's promise of guidance was not given so that we could avoid the strain of thinking. Indeed, John Wesley, the father of Methodism, said that God usually guided him by presenting reasons to his mind for acting in a certain way. This is important in every area – especially in the areas of marriage and jobs.

> **As we surrender our wills to God, He works in us and often changes our desires.**

Common sense is one of the factors to be taken into account in the area of choosing a life partner. It is common sense to look at - at least three very important areas.

i. **Spiritual Compatibility**

A Christian should only marry another Christian. Paul warns of the danger of marrying someone who is not a Christian (2 Corinthians 6:14). Spiritual compatibility means more than the fact both are Christians. It means that each party respects the other's spirituality, rather than simply being able to say, "at least they pass the test of being a Christian."

ii. **Personal Compatibility**

Obviously our marriage partner should be a very good friend and someone with whom there is a great deal in common. One of the many advantages of not having sex before marriage is that it is easier to concentrate on this area and discover whether or not there is personal compatibility. Often the sexual side if introduced will dominate the early stages of a relationship. If the foundation has not been built on friendship, then when the initial sexual excitement wears off it can leave the relationship with a very fragile basis.

> **our marriage partner should be a very good friend and someone with whom there is a great deal in common.**

iii. Physical Compatibility

This aspect is highlighting the need to be physically attracted to each other. It is not enough to be spiritually and emotionally compatible; the chemistry must be there as well. Often, the secular world makes the mistake of putting it first, but this should come last in the order of priorities.

4. Counsel of the Saints

The book of proverbs is full of injunctions to seek wise advice. The writer asserts that "a wise man listens to advice" (Proverbs 12:15). He warns that "plans fail for lack of counsel," but on the other hand, "with many advisers they succeed" (Proverbs 15:22). Therefore, he urges, "Make plans by seeking advice" (Proverbs 20:18).

While seeking advice it is very important, to always remember that ultimately our decisions are between us and God. They are our responsibility. We cannot shift that responsibility onto others or seek to blame them if things go wrong. The counsel of the saints is part of guidance – but it is not the only part. Sometimes it may be right to go ahead in spite of the advice of others.

> **It is not enough to be spiritually and emotionally compatible; the chemistry must be there as well.**

> **When we are faced with a decision where we need advice, we must choose our advisors carefully and prayerfully.**

When we are faced with a decision where we need advice, we must choose our advisors carefully and prayerfully. The best advisors are usually godly Christian people with wisdom and experience whom we respect. It is also good and wise to seek the advice of parents whom we are to honour, even if we are past the age of being under their authority and even if they are not Christians. This is because they know us very well and can often have important insights into situations.

5. Circumstantial Signs

God is in ultimate control of all events, the writer of Proverbs points out: *"in his heart a man plans his course, but the Lord determines his steps"* (Proverbs 16:9). Sometimes God opens doors and some other times He closes them. (1 Corinthians 16:9; Acts 16:7)

We might be praying about an issue and be running into or noticing certain coincidences, sometimes it may be God speaking to us through such coincidences.

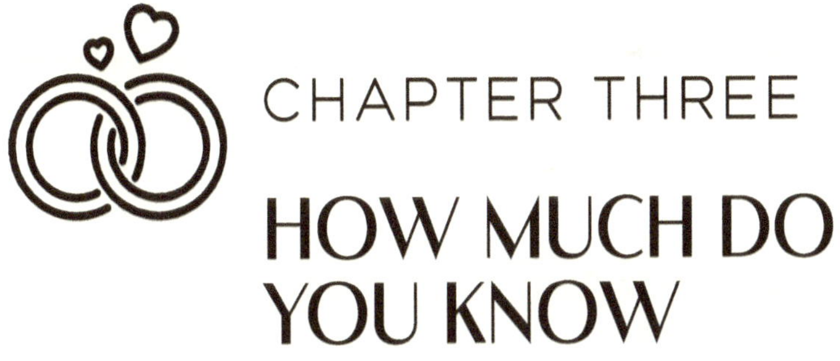

CHAPTER THREE

HOW MUCH DO YOU KNOW

How should you go about equipping and positioning yourself, to be able to offer something meaningful to another person's life as advocated in the previous chapter? Well, I'll put it straight – **find out!** The Bible says; "*…it is not good for a person to be without knowledge,…*"(Prov 19:2, NASB), so do yourself some good and go all out and acquire knowledge.

Find out about God and be in a relationship with him, this is the starting point. Find out and try to understand yourself, your gifts and abilities, your personality and your worldview. Find out about human nature and generally try to understand life and the world around

> **You must keep searching for knowledge, be curious and let sensible and relevant things interest you and urge you to seek answers.**

you, and how things work. Find out about the opposite sex and what a relationship with the opposite sex entails. Find out about marriage and what it means to get married and have a lasting relationship with one's spouse. Ask questions like, "Why are other couples able to live together for several decades but others are not?"You must keep searching for knowledge, be curious and let sensible and relevant things interest you and urge you to seek answers.

One way to gain knowledge is by going out to look for information. While there is a lot of information in the print media and online media –it takes discipline to put in the required effort and make the necessary sacrifice to get this information. Benjamin Franklin said, "Empty the coins in your purse into your mind and your mind will fill your purse with gold". You must always remember that no information that you will ever come across will ever be wasted. And you are better off having more information; (than you need), than lacking the information you need.

It is a good practice to find out things from trusted people who have the information you need. Every one of us can easily benefit from the 'accumulated experiences' of others. Creating opportunities to interact with parents, older people, senior colleagues, same-sex and opposite-sex friends can be very rewarding in equipping you for your future.

Getting Answers to the Knowledge You Seek from People

I am aware that getting information from people can be a daunting task for a good number of young people, because people don't just give out information, more often than not they require a secret fee, a fee that costs the giver absolutely nothing but rewards them abundantly. It helps him give a favourable impression and sells himself as a good conversationalist- the one people are excited to tell things. Dale Carnegie reveals this secret fee in his book *"How to win friends and influence people"*. He says *"Be a good listener..."*.

It is one thing to find out things from people but entirely another to do it in a way and attitude they can relate with. That is why you need to be a good listener and ask the kind of questions

And you are better off having more information; (than you need), than lacking the information you need.

> **Be a good listener and ask the kind of questions people will enjoy answering. Ask people questions, but most importantly, be an attentive listener.**

people will enjoy answering. Ask people questions, but most importantly, be an attentive listener. How can you do this?

Dale Carnegie paints a good picture of this in his writing about Dr Eliot. He says: "Dr Eliot's listening was not mere silence, but a form of activity. Sitting very erect on the end of his spine with hands joined in his lap, making no movement except that he revolved his thumbs around each other faster or slower, he faced his interlocutor and seemed to be hearing with his eyes as well as his ears. He listened with his mind and attentively considered what you had to say while you said it... at the end of an interview the person who had talked to him felt that he had had his say".

We shouldn't for any reason limit our friendships to only persons of the same sex with us. Thankfully the era of parents and guardians warning their wards against friendships with the opposite sex is long gone. More African parents are beginning to appreciate the value of inter-gender relationships to the emotional and social development of their children. I will ever be grateful to my father for exposing me to the truth, early in life - that:

'friendships with the opposite sex in itself isn't wrong, it is the engagement in any inappropriate conduct while relating with the opposite sex that makes it wrong and sinful, hence the need to set limits'. I will be discussing more on such limits later in the book.

> **We shouldn't for any reason limit our friendships to only persons of the same sex with us.**

CHAPTER FOUR

EQUIP YOURSELF

THERE IS A WIDE RANGE of issues that you need to sort out in your life before embarking on the journey of marriage. I was privileged to come across a great deal of information which helped me immensely. I encountered some of these issues through discussions with my biological father, my spiritual fathers and other elderly Christians and also through my reading of Christian literature. Here is a summary of some very important issues that you should address in your life before you start a romantic relationship with the opposite sex.

• Be Sure of Your Salvation

When asked the question "Are you born again?" and you are quick to say yes, are you sure of it? Are you absolutely sure that you are saved? Have you come to a point in your life where you totally believe in the death and resurrection of Jesus Christ and you have had the opportunity to confess your sins to Him and invite Him into your life to be your Lord and Saviour? And since then have you stopped living life on your terms but strictly on His terms through the direction of the Holy Spirit? Being sure of your salvation is important before you look towards marriage because you need your salvation experience and an ongoing relationship with the Lord Jesus Christ to cope with the challenges of marriage.

> **Have you come to a point in your life where you totally believe in the death and resurrection of Jesus Christ**

• Start Praying for a Life Partner Early in Life

You need to start praying for that person you hope to get married to. You sure don't know anything about him or her yet but it will be wise to talk to God about him/her. Ask God to shape and keep him/her for when He will bring you together.

Doing this also is building a habit; that will benefit both of you when you finally marry and start living together. It is something you will keep doing for as long as you live.

• Take Heed of Where to Look as You Search for a Life Partner

Knowing where to look and where not to look for a marriage partner is also of utmost importance. This too has to be thought through seriously and decided on in good time. And I make bold to say you are unlikely, almost impossible to find a godly partner in an ungodly environment.

• Focus on Working on Yourself

You need to keep working on your personality continuously. As a person, you know yourself better than anyone outside does, even if they make a claim to the contrary. Those personality flaws you have, have got to be worked upon by you.

Those personality flaws you have, have got to be worked upon by you.

If you don't work towards correcting them, they will get worse as you grow older and fuse into your

> **Your character and personality should really concern you, and working on them while you are still young should be a top priority.**

character and habits and by the time they begin to manifest in marriage, you will be sorry you ignored them.

Your character and personality should really concern you, and working on them while you are still young should be a top priority. It is worth mentioning here that, character is a makeup of our inborn nature plus our acquired habits. A person's character is said to be thirty percent nature and seventy percent habit. Generally, the character of a person over twenty years already contains more habit than nature and at over fifty years of age one already has a set personality with a definite pattern that has developed over the years. So, it goes to say, the earlier you appreciate the need to work on your character and begin doing it, the better. Fortunately, there is plenty of information in books on how to help yourself be a better person.

• Be Sure of Your Calling in Life

You were born for a purpose. You are not on Earth just to take up space. So a question you must ponder seriously is: do you know your purpose? Do you know what task

God has for you to accomplish in your generation? You need to sort this out before the question of who to marry can correctly be answered.

In Genesis chapter two, we read in verse 15 that "The Lord God took the man, and put him into the garden of Eden to dress it and keep it. God first assigned man a task before providing him with a helper. Thus we read in verse 18 that "The Lord God said, it is not good that the man should be alone; I will make him a help meet for him.

God has a task for you to do already but you need to ask him to make clear to you what it is. Knowing that before deciding who to spend your life with as a spouse will simplify the decision in very many ways, especially for you who are eager to do God's will.

• Do Not be Carried Away by Physical/ Outward Beauty

It is alright to look for physical attraction in the person you want to marry but making that the most important criterion is about the worst mistake you will make concerning the choice of a life partner. You must keep in mind that the physical features you see in that person will never be permanent. Age alone will erode them, then there is a possibility of an accident or illness disfiguring one's physical appearance.

> **You must keep in mind that the physical features you see in that person will never be permanent. Age alone will erode them...**

Nevertheless, there is a beauty that can never fade, the inner beauty- (character), which I just hinted at above. If you focus on and identify a person of good character, as against their physical good looks then you are already on your way to a happy and blessed marriage.

• Your Partner Should Share the Same Faith/Belief with You

There is so much diversity in our understanding of God and how we are supposed to worship and serve Him. This difference in how things should be done in relation to serving and worshiping God no doubt is the main reason behind the different denominations we have. I know as a matter of fact that some of these denominations forbid inter-denominational marriages; for justifiable reasons.

Young men and women should as much as possible look within their denominational circles for spouses. Doing so will take care of some basic belief clashes that might occur if that is ignored.

In cases where you've found someone of a different denomination and are both convinced of God's will for your union, it will be wise to put in serious efforts and reconcile your differing denominational beliefs and methods during your courtship before settling in for marriage. Of course, there will be the issue of who compromises more and who lets go of their denomination's membership. That needs to be sorted out between you in consultation with your families and spiritual mentors.

> **It will be wise to put in serious efforts and reconcile your differing denominational beliefs and methods during your courtship**

• Be Committed to Pleasing God and Living for Him

If you ask me what makes two married people remain faithful and true to each other, and with a firm resolve to make sure their marriage succeeds and brings out God's

> **Your words and actions towards your partner should be inspired by your love for God and your commitment to living for Him.**

glory, I will say it is their individual commitment to living their lives to please God.

Looking to each other to determine how you will respond or react to their words and actions will only keep you apart and disappointed. Your words and actions towards your partner should be inspired by your love for God and your commitment to living for Him.

• Have the Fear of God in Your Life

Closely related to the issue discussed above is the matter of having the fear of God in you. The Bible says, "The fear of the Lord is the beginning of wisdom..."(Prov. 9:10). The wisdom you need to treat your spouse right and be at your best in playing your role as a husband or wife will only come from the fear of God.

This is not an issue of seeing God as a wicked king who sits with gazing eyes to punish anyone who disobeys Him. Rather it is a reverent fear that acknowledges the fact that God is my maker and He knows how best I should go about things so I choose to follow His wisdom and live by His standards. I choose to do things the way He wants them done.

• Be Committed to Learning More About God

If you are going to live your lives to please God and have the fear of God in your life, you will need to commit to learning more about God every day. How much of God do you know? Are you often confused about what steps you need to take to please Him?

Committing to learning more about God will mean you are enthusiastic about studying the Bible, talking with Him regularly in prayer and fellowshipping with His other children regularly. These three Christian practices are none negotiable for a child of God who is willing to learn more about Him.

> **Be enthusiastic about studying the Bible, talking with Him regularly in prayer and fellowshipping with His other children regularly.**

CHAPTER FIVE

"...UNTIL IT SO DESIRES"

◇◇◇

I WAS FORTUNATE TO GET a piece of balanced information about how to relate with the opposite sex from my father at a very early age. As I related with it in mind, I came across Song of Songs 2:7 and quickly noticed that the verse is repeated word for word two times in the same book – in 3:5 and 8:4, i.e. ***"Daughters of Jerusalem, I charge you by the gazelles and by the does of the field: Do not arouse or awaken love until it so desires."***

Relating with the opposite sex can be fun and exciting. It affords one the opportunity to ask questions and receive straight and helpful answers. Robbie Castleman wrote that "A man and woman need to ask each other

> "We need to ask each other honest questions with no hidden agenda behind what we say."

questions about a viewpoint that may be wise to consider or feelings that the other may not naturally share." She goes on to say "We need to ask each other honest questions with no hidden agenda behind what we say."

Brothers and Sisters in the church should offer each other a safe place to be who we are, ask what we will and grow as women and men of God together. The sexual distinction was God's idea not just for marriage and procreation but for all relationships that reflect his image. And while there are several other benefits, there is also the likelihood of various dangers and sins which we must guard against. The scripture quoted above says "...***Do not arouse or awaken love until it so desires.***" What is the wise King Solomon (who wrote those words) saying?

R.W. Orr in New International Bible Commentary gives the following explanation:- "*The idyll closer with longing for the caresses of the beloved (2:6), but for this she must wait. This is the use made here of the earnest charge to the probably frivolous daughters of Jerusalem, Do not arouse or awaken love; i.e. beware of arousing passion prematurely; don't urge youth into behaviour for which the time has not yet come.*"

It is of utmost importance for us as we relate with members of the opposite sex to "beware of arousing passion prematurely, and of urging ourselves into behaviour for which the time has not yet come. The way to watch out against these includes:

> **Beware of arousing passion prematurely, and of urging ourselves into behaviour for which the time has not yet come.**

- **Avoid the tendency to spend too much (unwarranted) time with the opposite sex**

It's important to be purposeful in your meetings when you are spending time with the opposite sex. So a very important question to always ask is; why is he/she coming? Or why is he/she asking to see me? When the purpose of your meeting is accomplished, the meeting should be closed and you go your separate ways. When there's nothing definite to discuss or do together like homework or office task, then the devil starts putting ideas into your head that will lead to arousing passions prematurely.

- **Avoid the temptation to discuss in private**

It's very tempting and often more convenient to prefer to discuss with the opposite sex in private, but that

> **When the purpose of your meeting is accomplished, the meeting should be closed and you go your separate ways.**

tendency should be deliberately avoided. Discussing with the opposite gender should be always done in public spaces- whether in the school environment, work environment or at an eating place.

- ## Avoid reading and/or watching unchaste (erotic) content

Some of Satan's potent weapons are the screen, music and generally the media. He has inspired his agents to put out to the public, all manner of sex-provoking sounds and sights that are calculated to arouse your sexual passions and keep your thoughts on the subject until you go looking for ways to put to practice what you heard, read of or saw on some screen.

You will be doing yourself a lot of service by running away from anything that is not meant to build your spiritual life and encourage you in the way of the lord.

- **Take heed to your choice of words when talking with the opposite sex**

An objective way to check how your heart is faring in regard to the world's influence is to listen to what you let out of your mouth. The Bible says *"...out of the abundance of the heart the mouth speaketh"* (Matt. 12:34). When you find yourself voicing out to the opposite sex some lustful ideas or temptation-soaked words then you should quickly retrace your steps and seek help. That is a clear indication that your heart is tilted towards arousing passions prematurely; your passion has been aroused and you are on the verge of arousing the same in some other person.

> **When you find yourself voicing out to the opposite sex some lustful ideas or temptation-soaked words then you should quickly retrace your steps**

- **Don't have only opposite-sex friends, have close same-sex friends as well**

A lot of people confess to preferring friendship with the opposite sex and admit to being able to connect at a deeper level with the opposite sex; not necessarily for sinful reasons but they find that things worked out better in regards to friendship with the opposite sex than with their same sex friends.

For a young person, I will say this is not advisable and it is not healthy for you. You must make it a point of duty to have same-sex friends that you can spend time with every now and then. Opposite-sex friends should only complement your same-sex friends until you are ready to take steps towards a marriage relationship.

• **Avoid being idle; find something to do.**

Idleness is a terrible situation to be in and should be avoided by all means. Many evil and sinful thoughts were hatched at those idle moments when people sat doing nothing and allowed their thoughts to wander aimlessly. It is very wise to always engage both your hands and your mind in something productive and purposeful. The popular saying: an idle mind is the devil's workshop, holds true and is also consistent with biblical truth.

> **It is very wise to always engage both your hands and your mind in something productive and purposeful.**

• **Make it a priority to regularly create time for God and the things of God**

We live in a fast-paced world and always get busy trying to make ends meet. We try to live up to expectations of work or school or relationships so much so that we often neglect setting apart time to listen to God, either by reading the Bible, praying or attending church services and religious activities.

But anyone who is too busy to have time for these all-important activities on a regular basis is on the wrong path and will soon lose their way in this world. Because regularly engaging in these activities nourishes your spirit man as well as your soul and keeps you on the right path. These spiritual activities shouldn't be ignored for whatever reason if you want to stay safe on the right path and not arouse passions prematurely.

The list is in no way exhaustive, but you must be careful to know what to avoid, what not to overdo and what to do. In addition, be committed to avoiding tempting situations or being instruments of temptation to others.

> **Spiritual activities shouldn't be ignored for whatever reason if you want to stay safe on the right path and not arouse passions prematurely.**

CHAPTER SIX

LOVE CAN WAIT

◇◇

THE WORDS OF THE WISE king Solomon that we have considered in the previous chapter caution us but also hint at a truth that we can't just gloss over, the fact that a time will come when *"...it will so desire."* A time will certainly come when it will no longer be a question of arousing passion prematurely but it will be right by several standards to do something about that desire. The desire to start and nurture a godly relationship with the opposite sex that will culminate into marriage. This might involve three basic stages: friendship, courtship and marriage. But what time will it be right and appropriate to start working towards that direction?

> **You need to come to the point where you have built emotional, psychological, social and material capacity that makes you ready.**

I have pointed out that first: it must be when you are sure you have something to offer. Second, it must be when one is ready. Having something to offer is the first step but you need to come to the point where you have built emotional, psychological, social and material capacity that makes you ready. Such readiness should be with the understanding of the challenges that you are sure to face. Often times, relating with the opposite sex has some serious and genuine emotional, psychological, financial and time demands right at the friendship stage. These demands are bound to interfere with your other involvements. This is why it is not enough just to decide within oneself when to start a serious relationship with the opposite sex that will lead to marriage, but to ensure that one is prepared emotionally, psychologically, financially, and in all aspects of human development. Otherwise one will not be able to meet the demands of the relationship that leads to marriage.

Those Going for a University Degree

Given the peculiar challenges of our day and time, I will say that you should by all means avoid going into any relationship during your early school years. The early school years should be a period to focus on one's studies in order to lay a solid foundation in one's field of endeavour. These early years might mean the first three years or even the entire duration of a bachelor's degree. The idea is for you to minimise distractions and make sure you come out with a full grasp of your course of study and a good degree. In addition to your academic pursuits, it is important to know that this period is also a time to rigorously build yourself for life generally.

Another point to keep in mind is that young boys and girls who are just starting an academic course of study will need some time (as they make their way through such a course) to mature. A good number of young people who start romantic relationships at a too-early age end up breaking them for one reason or the other. This is not surprising because as people grow and mature, their interests, reasoning, aspirations, desires and under-standing also mature and change. That certainly affects some choices they may have already made. So if you take your time, rather than rush, you will make a more meaningful and informed decision about who to marry and when.

> **You should by all means avoid going into any relationship during your early school years.**

You Can be Ready Without a University Degree

Indeed, it is not every young person that will have the opportunity to enrol in a tertiary institution for some certificate. Some may take the way of learning a trade, and I will love to point out that the advice given above should apply here too. Making it your target to avoid the distractions that come with starting a relationship when you should be giving all your time and concentration to acquiring the necessary skill of the trade for which you have enrolled.

When you concentrate on securing your future, you will find it a lot easier to start and nurture a responsible and meaningful relationship with the opposite sex.

It pays to face first things first; concentrating on securing your future should come before selecting a life partner. I can assure you that when you concentrate on securing your future, you will find it a lot easier to start and nurture a responsible and meaningful relationship with the opposite sex.

PART 2

WORKING IT OUT

CHAPTER 7

CHOOSING THE RIGHT PERSON

CHOOSING A LIFE PARTNER IS one of the most important choices a person can make in their lifetime. Fortunately, a good number of youths know and appreciate the importance and seriousness of this decision and try to be careful about how they go about making this all-important decision. Yet some people still have the unfortunate experience of discovering shortly after they marry that their choice was ill-informed and wrong. But as you might be well aware, the consequences of such a mistake are better imagined than experienced.

There are so many men and women out there that are single and open to the idea of marriage. How can you

> **"To have clarity is to have direction; to see clearly what lies ahead of you, and to know how to navigate from point A to point B successfully."**

make a choice that you won't regret two, three, five, ten years down the road?

I have already discussed some issues that you should sort out about yourself before facing the issue of finding who to marry. It is important to watch out for those same issues in the person you intend to marry. But there is more. Here is a list of some basic character traits I believe you need to look out for in your prospective partner before you commit to marrying the person.

The man should be:

i. **Affectionate** – having affection or warm regard; tender, devoted, fond, earnest, ardent.

ii. **Patient** – content to wait if necessary; not losing one's temper while waiting; not bothered with having to wait; not unwilling to wait.

iii. **Clear-minded** – the physical, emotional, mental and spiritual state of acuity. It is a state in which you know who you are, what abilities you have and what you can accomplish with those abilities.

To have clarity is to have direction; to see clearly what lies ahead of you, and to know how to navigate from point A to point B successfully.
- Praise George

iv. **Magnanimous** – noble and generous in spirit, forgiving, large-hearted.

v. **Diligent** – with intense concentration, focus, and responsible regard. characterized by care and perseverance in carrying out tasks.

vi. **Humble** – having or showing a low estimate of one's importance; not proud, arrogant or assuming.

The woman should be:

i. **Genuine** - …not counterfeit, spurious, false or adulterated; authentic; real; natural; true; pure. Someone has said, one who is not genuine may be welcome by others initially but the welcome will not last. Over time, it is genuineness which gains people's hearts and inspires people's confidence.

ii. **Deep** – profound, having great meaning or import, but possibly obscure or not obvious.

iii. **Respectful** – An attitude of good consideration or high regard, good opinion, honour or admiration.

iv. **Gracious** – kind and warmly courteous, tactful, compassionate, indulgent, charming and graceful, elegant and with good taste.

v. **Submissive** – inclined or willing to submit to orders or wishes of others. Meekly obedient or passive.

vi. **Teachable** – willing to receive instruction or to learn; docile.

There is no guarantee that you will find any person with all these character traits. However, I recommend that:

i. As you look, you should strike a reasonable and wise compromise. I will say that, in the two sets mentioned above, humility for the man and teachability for the woman will be capable of bringing about all the other traits. The man who is humble enough to listen to his partner will well be on his way to being the husband any woman will be happy to marry. And the teachable woman will be well on her way to making her man a proud and fulfilled husband.

> **Humility for the man and teachability for the woman will be capable of bringing about all the other traits.**

ii. In your preparation, you should work at developing and building these character traits into your personality, because with just these few basics you can be sure that living with anyone in a lifelong relationship will be easy and fun.

Above all...

The person you will settle for should demonstrate a convincing love for God and fear Him. I have mentioned this point about the fear of God in chapter 4, as an important issue to address in your personal life and now I am saying this is something to also make sure you see in the person you are considering for marriage. I see the love of God and the fear of God as two sides of a coin, especially in this context. And it is my strong recommendation that you watch out for this trait even more keenly than those earlier mentioned.

As important as looking out for these character traits may be, it should never be a substitute for being absolutely sure of God's leading and guidance. This I must say, is one area of my life that I have come to appreciate the truth God spoke through prophet Isaiah and said:-

**Above all...
The person
you will settle
for should
demonstrate a
convincing love
for God and
fear Him.**

"For my thoughts are not your thoughts, neither are your ways my ways, saith the LORD" (Isaiah 55:8). This is the basis for my saying what is most important is to be sure of God's leading and guidance in the steps you take on the issue of choosing a life partner. His guidance might often not be meaningful or logical to us by our human standards but if you are wise, you will follow Him without reservations or doubts.

The Psalmist tells us the way to securing God's leading and guidance in our lives, He says: *"Commit everything you do to the LORD, trust him, and he will help you."*(Psalm 37:5 NLT). The Amplified version put's it this way; *"commit your way to the Lord, (roll and repose each care of your load on Him): trust (lean on, rely on and be confident) also in Him and He will bring it to pass."*

> **I see the love of God and the fear of God as two sides of a coin, especially in this context. And it is my strong recommendation that you watch out for this trait even more keenly...**

As you diligently seek God's guidance and absolutely trust Him; be confident that he has your interest at heart in what he guides you to or brings your way, you will have no regrets whatsoever about the outcome. He says *"For I know the thoughts and plans that I have for you, says the Lord, thoughts and plans for welfare and peace and not for evil, to give you hope in your final outcome."* (Jeremiah 29:11, AMP). Is Him and His perfect will the burning desire of your heart? If it is then "he will help you"- he will guide you, and you will know that he has done it.

When it's all been said and done, nothing matters more in life than the assurance that you are in God's will for your life. When doubts arise and fears assail, - and that will surely happen in many areas of life. Sometimes it goes beyond a feeling, it's an experience of a series of challenges and hard times, your only antidote for regrets at that time is an unshakeable assurance that you are in God's will. It is only then that you can confidently say like Fanny Crosby; *"For I know whate'er befall me, Jesus doeth all things well"*.

CHAPTER EIGHT

RIGHT WOO, RIGHT RESPOND

IN CHAPTER SIX, I HAVE pointed out that the right time to start considering and taking steps towards a long-term relationship is when you have secured your future and are on track towards actualizing your dreamed future. When that is taken care of, I will expect the guy to start the process of wooing a lady who he possibly has been friends with and has seen in her certain character traits that he admires. You are wooing her by trying to communicate to her certain love gestures that tell her you love her and want a Marriage relationship with her. These gestures are targeted at convincing her about your love and affection for her so she can accept to embark on the love's journey of starting a relationship with you.

In a similar light, a lady too after being clear about where she is headed and setting her mind and effort on the track towards her dreamed future should have nothing to hold her back from entertaining advances from the opposite sex gender who are coming to you with an honest intention of a long-lasting relationship.

Winning a lady's heart can indeed be a daunting task and persistence might sometimes do the magic but for sure not always. At other times it will be smarter to check how one is going about it because some people ruin their chances of success by taking the wrong steps which they call persistence.

In most African cultures, males are the ones expected to make advances towards the ladies, therefore it will be a good thing for a young man to be conversant with the right way to approach this very important phase so he doesn't do it wrongly or frivolously. You might want to try things like appreciating her, throwing complimentary comments about what she puts on and does, spending time with her, especially on outings and showing genuine interest in her, her family,

> **...it will be a good thing for a young man to be conversant with the right way to approach this very important phase so he doesn't do it wrongly or frivolously.**

her friends, her career, her occupation and whatever she is involved in. This is absolutely important.

Guys will also need to watch out against things like lavishing someone you are just getting to know with expensive gifts and often talking about your personality and your accomplishments. You will need to be careful with the kind of gift you give to a lady at the time of wooing her. Gifts, at those times, if they must be given, should be simple items that will express your interest in their intellectual, career and spiritual development.

> **Watch out against things like lavishing someone you are just getting to know with expensive gifts and often talking about your personality...**

Most importantly, make time to be with her, not in a way that will distract her or lead you into necking and petting and fornication. A quick check on her at work and taking her out for a meal or a movie or some fun activity will certainly be appreciated by most ladies if not all.

You should also note that this wooing stage is a time to pay attention and try to figure out what the lady whose heart you are trying to win really appreciates and understands as love gestures. Find out from her or experiment with gestures and gifts that will leave no doubts in her heart

> **Find out from her or experiment with gestures and gifts that will leave no doubts in her heart about your genuine love and care for her.**

about your genuine love and care for her. I don't expect you to know all about treating a woman correctly, but I expect you to have a genuine concern for her as a person. Do it in a way she won't help noticing that you really care about her and all that concerns her.

In addition, I will say to the person who has some wooing to do, be yourself, know the right things to do and do them in your own way. Don't try to impress your lady with lies and empty promises. And above all, follow God's leading that you sense in your heart. When you have done what you can do and still haven't succeeded, you will have to let go and trust God for someone else.

Don't aim at impressing rather show genuine interest. I know that the temptation to impress someone you are interested in can be real and understandable, but you must remember that it takes you nowhere near getting the person's attention, let alone winning their affection. I found some very useful insights about this from *Dale Carnegie* that I will share with you. He says;

"If you want others to like you, if you want to develop real friendships, if you want to help others at the same time as yourself,... become genuinely interested in other people".

This works based on the fact that people are interested first in themselves. *Dale Carnegie* points out that "people are not interested in you. They are not interested in me. They are interested in themselves – morning, noon and after dinner".

> **If you want others to like you, if you want to develop real friendships, if you want to help others at the same time as yourself,... become genuinely interested in other people".**

Carnegie puts it, this way "People...are a hundred times more interested in themselves and their wants and problems than they are in your problems. A person's toothache means more to that person than a famine in China which kills a million people. A boil on one's neck interests one more than forty earthquakes in Africa". If we merely try to impress people and get people interested in us, we will not only fail but will never have any true, sincere relationships. Friends, real friends, are not made that way.

Ladies, please do not make things unnecessarily difficult.
I also have a few words for ladies. Please, ladies, try to help your man do things to you correctly. You should be

> **Be careful not to jump at a man's advances hastily, so he does not take advantage of your excitement about him.**

polite and honest in pointing out shortfalls to him, and allow him some time to do things differently. Do not compare him with other men and criticise to condemn him. Try to see the good things in him and appreciate his little efforts towards trying to win your affection.

As a lady, always be sincere to yourself. If you are interested in someone, there's no point pretending and giving him a different impression. You can find a way to encourage a person who is wooing you to keep up his attempts and allow you a little more time to sort yourself out. Doing that certainly serves you better than liking him in your heart and acting as though you are not interested at all.

You will however want to be careful not to jump at a man's advances hastily, so he does not take advantage of your excitement about him. At the same time, watch out against sending away someone you will want to keep.

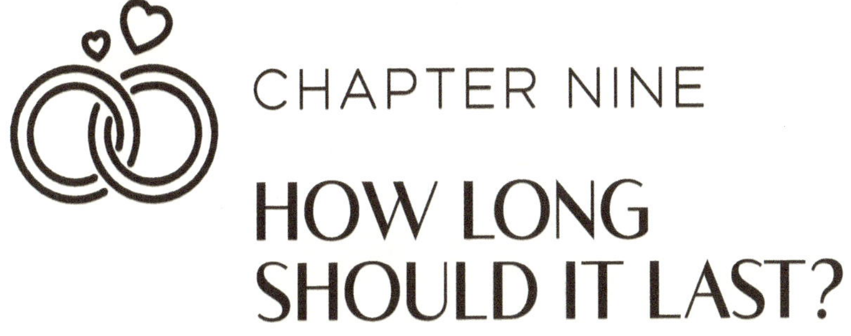

CHAPTER NINE

HOW LONG SHOULD IT LAST?

ONE QUESTION WHICH IS ON the mind of two people who are working their way towards a lasting relationship is the question of how long a courtship should last before they settle down for marriage. I am careful not to state an outright duration that a courtship should last because each has its peculiarities. I will rather emphasise what you should aim to achieve in a courtship relationship. To that effect I will say, aim at knowing those basic things about the other person that will help you make up your mind about them and possibly lay aside a little time after gaining that knowledge to get acquainted with yourselves as you discuss. That will help you ascertain whether you are willing to live with that person for a

> **Aim at knowing those basic things about the other person that will help you make up your mind about them and possibly lay aside a little time after gaining that knowledge to get acquainted with yourselves.**

lifetime or not. When you are certain that those fundamental things about your would-be partner are well known to you, then you will need to answer this question; "Am I willing to live with this person for the rest of my life?"

There is no justification for an unnecessarily long courtship. I say so because of the high likelihood of a long court-ship sliding into an unholy affair. If you think you will survive long courtships because your parents did so in their days, then you must think again.

You must accept the reality that we are living in times when life is a lot more challenging than it was for our parents when they were growing up. What worked for them in their time might hardly work for us now. For instance, my father got married to my mother when he was 25 years old. Most people will agree with me that today, marrying at that age is almost impossible for someone who is going to be the one to fend for his family. I also desired to marry at the age of 25 years but delays in school due to strikes made me stay longer in school than was necessary, and it was clear to me at a point how impossible realising that target was going to be. Thankfully, by God's special grace, I ended up marrying just a year off that target but it still wasn't as easy as it probably was with my father.

During our parents' days, they didn't experience delays in schools due to strikes the way we have it now. In their time employment was guaranteed for any graduate, unlike it is in our time. Then there's the issue of the cost implication of marrying, both in terms of dowry payment and church wedding expenses. All these aspects of marriage were not as costly for our parents as they are with us now. These and other implications are the realities of our time which it will be wise to consider as we set out to plan and decide when we will start and nurture a relationship for marriage.

These are some of the issues young people must seriously contemplate and be sure of how they will cope with and navigate them, before deciding when to commence a relationship and determining how long a courtship would last.

There is no justification for an unnecessarily long courtship. I say so because of the high likelihood of a long courtship sliding into an unholy affair.

A Focused and Purposeful Courtship

I have thoughtfully come to the conclusion that courtship should not be shorter than six months and not longer than two years. Its actual duration should depend on the peculiar circumstances of the people involved in the relationship. As well as how committed both of you are in putting in concerted efforts towards knowing each other enough to make up your minds about starting life as husband and wife.

A focused and purposeful courtship is one that you both are committed to the goal of knowing each other better, (in order to help you make an informed decision about your future together), a high priority. In which case, you make certain that all the time you spend together whether in person, on the phone or on chats serve the purpose of trying to know each other better. As you watch, ask questions and respond to each other, you are listening carefully and getting clues that will help you know and understand the other person better.

> **I have thoughtfully come to the conclusion that courtship should not be shorter than six months and not longer than two years.**

The aim is to acquaint yourselves with each other's personalities. This requires a sincere commitment from both parties to be totally honest and open with no iota of pretence or lies. When you give this kind of wholehearted commitment to your courtship, it will lead you to a point in your relationship when it will become clear to you that it is time to start making marriage plans. That conviction in your heart has to be backed up by a word from God as confirmation for you to go ahead to start the marriage preparations.

> **This requires a sincere commitment from both parties to be totally honest and open with no iota of pretence or lies.**

LAY A SOLID FOUNDATION

THE MOST IMPORTANT INVESTMENT YOU can ever make in your relationship is to lay a solid foundation for it. Laying the right foundation is your only guarantee for a relationship that will last and be fulfilling. Unfortunately, many young people don't give the foundational years of their relationship the attention and commitment it requires they choose to go about it flippantly.

The importance of a foundation can be better appreciated when you take a close look at its function in a building. It is a well-known fact even by non-professionals in the building industry that the most important part of any building is its foundation. It is the foundation that

> **Laying the right foundation is your only guarantee for a relationship that will last and be fulfilling.**

gives the building its strength and stability. That is why when constructing a building, more attention is given to the foundation than its visible portions. So for the most part, it is often quite easy to tell the problem whenever a building collapses.

The same principle applies to human relationships, especially romantic ones. There's got to be a good enough foundation if it is to stand the test of time. A solid foundation is key to maintaining all the thrill and passion that brought you together. Here are seven foundational blocks you must put in place for your relationship if you want it to stand the test of time.

1. Be Best friends

Laying a foundation of true friendship is so vital that for a long time, I contemplated making it the main foundation ingredient and let the other aspects I will be discussing come as subtopics to it. And note that I am not talking about just being true friends but being "best of friends".

Best friends share a bond that is deeper and stronger than regular friends. It is a bond that keeps them together and keeps them dear to one another no matter the odds they come against.

In Prov. 18:24, we read this very enlightening thing about friendship, it says: ***"There are friends who pretend to be friends, but there is a friend who sticks closer than a brother"*** (RSV). Laying a foundation of "best friends" means being that friend that sticks closer than a brother.

2. Know How to Touch Each Other's Heart

Once you've both made up your minds for a relationship, your next task is to understudy and know as much as you possibly can about the other person. One of the most important things you should know about your partner is how to communicate the love you feel for him/her in a way that will be understood as such, accepted and meaningful to them.

When you know this about your partner, you will need to make use of that knowledge several times a day for every day of your lives together. Human beings indeed

> **One of the most important things you should know about your partner is how to communicate the love you feel for him/her**

change but this is one aspect of a person's make-up that hardly ever changes.

3. Be Real

There shouldn't be an occasion for you to speak or behave outside your real self. There is always that temptation to put up a front in speech and behaviour that is only targeted at impressing your partner and making him/her see you in a certain way. You must resist that temptation. Instead, choose to always be yourself.

> **Being yourself... affords your partner the opportunity to know you for who you really are and make an informed decision as to whether or not you are the kind of person he/she wants.**

Being yourself does not in any way mean everything about your personality is unquestionable, no! But it affords your partner the opportunity to know you for who you really are and make an informed decision as to whether or not you are the kind of person he/she wants. Also, being yourselves helps each of you to see and note what areas of your lives need blending. Taking note of such areas is a vital step towards figuring out possible ways of how to go about it.

4. Stay in Touch

You also need to lay a foundation for good and effective communication. Being able to freely express your thoughts, feelings and needs to the other person is very important and needs to be attained at all costs. One way to go about attaining that is by making efforts to always keep in touch. Just keep in touch and talk about "sweet nothings".

It is important to note that a major hindrance to free-flowing communication is keeping secrets from your partner. Do you have things to hide from your partner? If you do, you can be sure that you cannot achieve or attain the kind of communication I am advocating. Avoiding secrets makes way for both of you to always have something to talk about and to do so in great depth.

It is imperative for you two to undertake never to hold back anything from the other person. And this involves not holding back both your pleasant and unpleasant feelings about things said and done to you. Instead, learn to express yourselves politely and courteously to teach other.

> **Being able to freely express your thoughts, feelings and needs to the other person is very important and needs to be attained at all costs.**

5. Be a Team

Another foundation stone you must put in place is to always see yourselves as a two-man team that desperately needs the other person to succeed. This is where the popular phrase "life partner" needs to be emphasised.

> **See yourselves as a two-man team that desperately needs the other person to succeed.**

You are partners that need to work side by side to achieve success in your relationship. This means nothing is undertaken without first consulting with the other person. You don't take decisions on your own, you always discuss and arrive at decisions together, and as much as possible; do things together.

6. Avoid Any Form of Physical Intimacy

One of the worst enemies of a successful and God honouring marriage is physical intimacy during courtship. The temptation to get physically intimate is real and hard to resist. Unfortunately, many have found reasons to rationalize and justify physical intimacy during courtship. They forget that God's instructions for us to flee youthful lusts and not fornicate are actually for our good.

Venturing into any form of physical intimacy gets in the way of both of you developing intimacy in other non-physical ways that are needful and more helpful in guaranteeing the success of your marriage.

Of course, your hormones don't have time for such wisdom, when they start screaming for some intimate touch and they can easily lure you to fornication if you have not learned to respect the boundaries set around physical intimacy. I will be offering practical suggestions on how to get a hold of our sex desires and urges in chapters 13 and 14.

7. Be Constantly Learning and Growing

You can never reach a point in your life when you have learned everything there is to learn, hence the need to make it a priority to keep learning. You need to keep building your knowledge base.

Fortunately, there is an unhindered access to great knowledge out there; people are highly willing to share their experiences and anyone with a willing heart will

> **Keep building on that knowledge layer by layer to ensure that you improve your way of relating with your partner.**

always have access to some relevant knowledge to learn from and get better.

It is very foolish and destructive to stay with the knowledge you had when you started out in a relationship. You have got to keep building on that knowledge layer by layer to ensure that you improve your way of relating with your partner.

This learning should include reaching out to know and understand your partner better and better and also acquiring relevant relationship skills that will help your interactions with each other be more fun and meaningful.

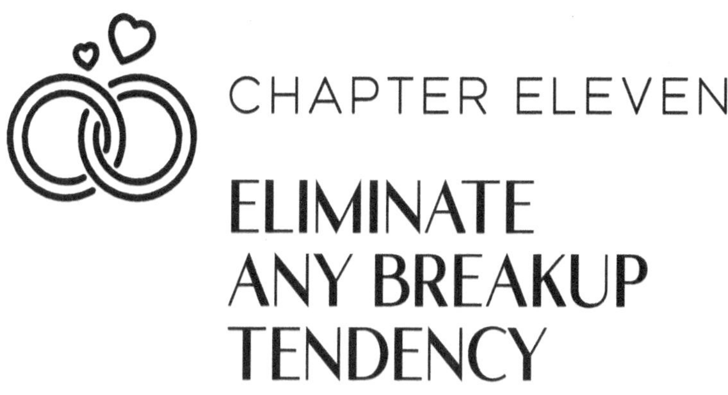

CHAPTER ELEVEN

ELIMINATE ANY BREAKUP TENDENCY

AS WE ADVANCE IN KNOWLEDGE and technology, the issue of making our relationships stand the test of time seems to be getting more complex and out of reach for many people. It seems for many single youths it is a normal thing to be involved in many relationships before you finally settle down with a life partner. But this is not normal and should never be seen or accepted as the norm. This is particularly expedient considering the devastation broken relationships bring to lives. Some people took to promiscuity as a result of a broken relationship and for some, a breakup turned them into enemies while

> **Breakups very often result from avoidable disagreements.**

for others, a certain breakup left them emotionally and psychologically shattered to the point of giving up on being loved or giving out love.

Breakups very often result from avoidable disagreements. These though avoidable, may come in ways no one expects, and threaten the peace and stability in your relationship. It is my strong conviction that it is possible to have fewer and fewer conflicts in our relationships until it is conflicts free. Paying attention to the following four issues will go a very long way in guaranteeing some stability and eliminating any breakup tendency;

1. No Premature Commitment

It is very unwise to be hasty in making decisions concerning long-lasting relationship matters. The fact that you are praying and working towards making your relationship last for a lifetime alone should make you consider issues very carefully and prayerfully before deciding on them.

2. Focus on Developing True Friendship First

Psychologists widely agree that love has two primary components. Namely;

- **Passionate- erotic love** – physical intimacy and sexual desire for a person.

- **Companionate love** – friendship-type platonic love towards a person.

It is obvious that many people spend time nursing the erotic love, which in reality should come last in order of priorities. That is why I am stressing here that you must deliberately put in the required efforts to develop the second component – "companionate love" – first.

> **Many people spend time nursing the erotic love, which in reality should come last in order of priorities.**

This period of developing companionate love also allows each of you to see how the other person fits into your life and especially your future as you conceive it to be.

3. Ensure to Have a Regular Review of Your Relationship

Let there be a regular assurance given to each other about how committed you both are to the relationship. It is possible that once in a while or on several occasions some misunderstanding or distance may threaten to weaken the passion you felt when you started. When you notice any emotional distance between you or some indifference from the other person, you will need to set out time to talk about the state of the relationship and verbally express your commitment to each other and to the relationship.

You must watch out against being too stereotypic in how you go about it. You must be sure to express the truth that you see and feel about the condition of the relationship in clear and unambiguous terms. And follow up by giving assurance to each other that, despite that, you will still give your one hundred percent commitment to the relationship and to seeing that things work out to the best.

> **Let there be a regular assurance given to each other about how committed you both are to the relationship.**

4. Have a Right Attitude Towards Disagreements

Disagreements are bound to occur between people who try to live or work together, no matter how hard they try to avoid it. As bad as they may be or sound, disagreements are not bad in themselves if handled properly. They can strengthen your relationship if you positively harness the lessons they bring along. You can't expect to progress in your knowledge of the next person that you relate with if you try to avoid disagreements. You should learn to see disagreements in a positive light; as great opportunities to grow in your knowledge of each other and your relationship.

There are different ways people approach disagreements and each approach has its inherent result. Most of the following insights are excerpts from a "pre-marriage counselling manual" which Mr David Tyokighir used to counsel me and my wife during our courtship.

> **Learn to see disagreements in a positive light; as great opportunities to grow in your knowledge of each other**

Different Approaches in Handling Conflict/Disagreement

1. **Must win** - You must have the last word; you must be in charge.

   Results:

   a. Kills communication and eventually destroys the relationship.

   b. you win (you protect your pride) but you lose (the closeness and respect of your partner).

2. **Withdraw or Yield** – you back off or give in whenever a disagreement begins.

   Results:

   a. you have kept the peace but;
      i. have buried your needs.
      ii. have deprived your partner of your ideas and opinions.

   b. the relationship is being damaged;
      i. distance increases rather than closeness.
      ii. misunderstanding remains rather than understanding being gained.

   c. you are teaching your partner that;
      i. Your opinions and needs are not important
      ii. he or she can always have his or her way.

3. **Negotiate** – you give up something in order to gain something; you negotiate.

Results:

   a. negotiating may not build oneness and understanding.

   b. you remain opponents rather than becoming partners.

   c. selfishness is not dealt with.

4. **Resolve** – you find an answer together; you solve the problem.

Results:

   a. you both grow in love and self-sacrifice by putting the other's needs first.

   b. you give up some of what you wanted, but you do it willingly to strengthen your relationship, save the relationship from breakup and add to your understanding of each other.

I must point out that the best approach, i.e. **"Resolve"**, will for most people be the most difficult approach, but we must for our relationship's sake strive to make it our natural approach towards handling disagreements.

But how does this work?

How to Go About Resolving Conflicts/ Disagreements

1. Let go of any angry feelings and take a close look at the cause of the disagreement.

---

2. Make up your mind to have the matter resolved.

---

3. Find a good time to talk about the problem. The earlier you address the problem the better, don't let disagreements pile up, but make sure both of you are ready to discuss the issue. The Bible admonishes us not to let the sun go down on our anger. (Eph. 4:26)

---

4. Sit together and talk – start by hearing each other out on what each one thinks really went wrong and highlighting why it made you angry. Attack the problem, not each other. Be very polite so you don't worsen the situation.

---

5. Discuss possible practical solutions, their implications on each of you and the challenges involved in each case.

---

6. Discuss what you can both do to prevent any re-occurrence.

---

7. Discuss your feelings and try to evaluate each other's reactions and its implication on the relationship.

---

8. Forgive each other. Forgiveness is not a feeling but something you choose to do.

---

9. Hug or shake each other.

Let God's Will Prevail

It will be important to add that, sometimes breaking up is the wise thing to do. Our discussion in this chapter has been to guide you into making sure that a breakup doesn't happen because of some minor misunderstanding. But it is okay to break up when it becomes clear that, your relationship is not God's perfect will for your life. When you get such a conviction through prayer and a clear word from God then the wise thing to do is for the two of you to go your separate ways. And probably just be friends.

Joshua Harris puts it this way: Courtship is a season for two people to grow in friendship, to get to know each other's character and to see how they interact as a couple. It is also a

> **But it is okay to break up when it becomes clear that, your relationship is not God's perfect will for your life.**

time to consider the possibility of marriage and to seek to make a wise choice. Some courtships end with two people deciding that they should remain friends.

CHAPTER TWELVE

STAY WITHIN LOVING LIMIT

MANY SINGLES HAVE QUESTIONS ABOUT their limits in relating to the opposite sex. They want to know what is acceptable and what is not. Even those in courtship are asking similar questions and are eager to know the boundaries to the expression of affection among themselves; they sincerely wonder how far is too far.

Many writers have offered useful guides that I find very meaningful. Dean Sherman addressing the question of "how far is too far?" draws attention to two scriptural references viz:

i. *"Everything is permissible for me"- but not everything is beneficial. "Everything is permissible for me" - but I will not be mastered by anything.* (1 Corinthians 6:12)

ii. *"Everything is permissible" –but not everything is beneficial. "Everything is permissible" – but not everything is constructive. Nobody should seek his own good, but the good of others.* (1 Corinthians 10:23-24)

He points out that there is a need to objectively evaluate everything you do in a relationship according to three simple questions: **Is it right? Is it loving? Is it wise?**

From my interactions with singles, I have found that many interpret the above question subjectively and rationalize wrong actions based on wrong information they have acquired from various sources. I find Apostle Paul's admonition to Timothy a yet more straightforward and practical guide. Paul wrote to Timothy that *"treat ... younger women as sisters, with absolute purity."* (1 Timothy 5:1-2). It is quite

> **A quick way for objective evaluation would be to honestly answer the question: "Will I be glad to do this with my biological sister or brother"?**

easy for most people to identify with culturally acceptable limits when relating to their biological siblings. Paul told Timothy and it is for you to apply those same limits to your relationship with the opposite sex. A quick way for objective evaluation would be to honestly answer the question: *"Will I be glad to do this with my biological sister or brother"?*

> **my expression of affection to him/her should not be different from how I do it to my biological brother/sister.**

I agree with writers and speakers that make it abundantly clear that it is important for two people in courtship to express their affection to each other. But what I believe will help them stay within godly loving limits is the consciousness that this person remains my brother/sister until when we marry. Therefore, my expression of affection to him/her should not be different from how I do it to my biological brother/sister.

Joshua Harris addressing this issue in the context of courtship points out that any Christian courtship must be governed and guided by the understanding that you two are *More than Friends but Less than Lovers*. He goes further to say;

"The priority of a God-glorifying, wisdom-guided courtship should be;

    i.   To treat each other with holiness and sincerity

    ii.   To make an informed and wise decision about marriage.

These two priorities must however be pursued with two very important goals:

    i.   To grow

    ii.   To guard.

You want to grow closer so you can truly know each other's character, but you also want to guard each other's hearts because the outcome of your relationship is still unknown. The fact that the future is unknown should motivate you to treat each other with the kind of integrity that will allow you to look back on your courtship without regret, regardless of the outcome.

> **Guard each other's hearts because the outcome of your relationship is still unknown.**

Maintaining the priorities of growing and guarding makes courtship something of a balancing act. You have a clear purpose to consider marriage, but you also need to fight the urge to assume that you're going to get married.

You could say that in courtship we're walking across the high wire stretched between friendship and marriage. The two priorities of growing and guarding are like the two ends of our balancing pole. We need to hold our pole in the middle for success. If we're too guarded, we won't move forward in the relationship; if we grow close too fast, we risk emotional injury or unwise choices.

> **You could say that in courtship we're walking across the high wire stretched between friendship and marriage. The two priorities of growing and guarding are like the two ends of our balancing pole.**

You're more than friends, so you can determine whether you should join your lives in marriage, but you are less than lovers – your hearts and bodies don't yet belong to each other."

However you understand and take the suggestions above, it will do you a lot of good and help you avoid unnecessary clashes with your opposite-sex friend if you discuss this issue and let him/her know where you stand on this question of acceptable loving limits. Discussing this will help you in at least three ways;

i. Helps you know what to expect and what not to expect.

---

ii. Helps you not to violate or abuse the other person in any way imaginable.

---

iii. Helps you honour God in your relationship.

CHAPTER THIRTEEN

NO PLACE FOR SEX

ONE OF THE MOST DARING issues that challenge young people in relationships with the opposite sex is sexual temptation. And because our generation is more exposed to sex than past generations, many young people are inclined to experiment with it at any given opportunity.

There is a lot out there that keeps throwing sex at you, it is almost as if one can't escape from sex scenes. Pornography is common on the Internet, in magazines and some TV adverts and programs expose viewers to sex unsolicited. Sex hits at us with an overwhelming force. Our generation perfectly identifies with the lines, "I see

> **You must however keep in mind that pre-marital and extra-marital sex have consequences that are real and severe.**

the sights that dazzle, the tempting sounds I hear", by a hymn writer.

You must however keep in mind that pre-marital and extra-marital sex have consequences that are real and severe. Above all, you must always remember that God's standards regarding sex are still unchanged and are put down for your good and in your best interest. It highly behoves you to strive to uphold God's standards without any excuses. I have found a few insights that were of tremendous help to me in my relationship with the opposite sex in my single years.

Discipline Your Heart and Mind

You must grow to a point where you don't give a second thought to anything ungodly. I believe the road to that is taking in God's word and meditating on it- regularly thinking about it. Apostle Paul admonishes us to *"Let the word of God dwell in you richly as you teach and admonish one another with all wisdom, and as you sing psalms, hymns and spiritual songs with gratitude in your hearts to God"* [Colossians 3:16 (NLT)].

The temptation to sin starts within you, in your heart and mind. The devil suggests a thought and when you ponder on it, you end up carrying it out. It, however, always starts with just a single thought. Jesus spoke to the Pharisees and Teachers of the law about inner purity and said this: "But what comes out of the mouth gets its start in the heart.

"It's from the heart that we vomit up evil arguments, murders, adulteries, fornications, thefts, lies, and cussing" [Matt 15:18-19 (MSG)].

You read the following words from James: *"The temptation to give in to evil comes from us and only us. We have no one to blame but the leering, seducing flare-up of our own lust. Lust gets pregnant, and has a baby: sin! Sin grows up to adulthood, and becomes a real killer"* [James 1:14-15 (MSG)].

You must discipline your heart and mind, and the way to do that is by expunging any evil thoughts that the devil brings. Don't dwell on it, just dispel it or better still, hold it captive to the obedience of Christ, as apostle Paul admonishes: "We use our powerful God-tools for smashing warped philosophies, tearing down barriers erected against

> **The temptation to sin starts within you, in your heart and mind.**

> **You must discipline your heart and mind, and the way to do that is by expunging any evil thoughts that the devil brings**

the truth of God, fitting every loose thought and emotion and impulse into the structure of life shaped by Christ" [2 Cor 10:5 (MSG)].

There are three ways that you can work with your heart and mind to overcome sexual temptation.

1. Think about your future

The urge for sex comes so strongly that it is most times difficult to think straight at such moments, but you can strive even at those tense moments to think of the future and how honouring to God it will be to never give in at that point and wait a little longer. Think of the necessity to delay it a little longer. The truth is, such tense moments only last a couple of seconds- few minutes at most.

2. Direct your thoughts to something else

The best will be to call to memory some important Bible verses at such tense moments, but other than that you must deliberately take your thoughts off sex and direct them to something else of interest to you.

3. Get your hands on something

Sometimes it might not be easy to direct your thoughts to some other thing, but it will sure be easier to find something to do. Not just something you will do superficially, but something that you can give all your physical energy and mental attention to do.

Discipline Your Body and Senses

This aspect focuses on what you put your eyes and your ears to. Pornography is one such thing that you must discipline yourself to run away from. Colin Peckham describes pornographic magazines and lurid videos as a totally selfish comfort zone which weakens one's whole moral fibre and hastens the drift from spirituality and also makes you vulnerable to temptation. The same applies to worldly music.

Pornography is one such thing that you must discipline yourself to run away from.

I checked out the meaning of the word 'discipline' in the Encarta dictionary and I was endeared to the meaning that says: "the ability to behave in a controlled and calm way even in a difficult or stressful situation". Of a truth, you will certainly find yourself in difficult and stressful situations, situations that tempt you to disobey and dishonour God. Thankfully, God

Having Jesus in your life is the first step to being able to behave in a controlled and calm way

has made available the ability you need to stay calm and controlled in the face of those situations, and that can be found in Jesus Christ, through the power of the Holy Spirit.

Having Jesus in your life is the first step to being able to behave in a controlled and calm way, even in difficult and stressful situations. The second step is doing it. This is where you decide to put that ability to use. This one comes from you. God will not come down and do it for you. Apostle Paul said *"I discipline my body like an athlete, training it to do what it should. Otherwise, I fear that after preaching to others I myself might be disqualified"* (1 Cor. 9:27). God has already done His part and you must do yours, so go for it- discipline yourself.

Set Clear Relationship Boundaries

Relationships with the opposite sex must be preceded by a clearly defined boundary that will help you stay sexually pure as we have said earlier. Dean Sherman points us to the scripture in Galatians 5:19 and 2 Corinthians 12:2 where an uncommon word LASCIVIOUSNESS is used. He says lasciviousness can be defined as "stirring up within us or within another person, desires that cannot be righteously satisfied." He says further that "we can stir up sexual desires by touching someone or looking at someone in a suggestive way. Wearing revealing clothes, walking in a certain way, dancing a certain way, and saying things with a double meaning can all count as lascivious behaviour if they are done to stir up sexual desire that cannot be fulfilled in ourselves or another person. The key here is intention.

> **"It is wise to agree on the limit of time, talk and touch at every stage of a romantic relationship before the need for them arises.**

Robbie Castleman also offers some very useful safeguards for sexual conduct and spells out four simple rules. She says "It is wise to agree on the limit of time, talk and touch at every stage of a romantic relationship before the need for them arises. It is much harder to think clearly, assert your will or slow things down in the middle of increasing passion. Human sexual appetite is too powerful to trust to a 'see –what –to –do – as –we –go –along strategy." Her suggested rules are:

Rule 1: **Four feet on the floor!**

The appetite for sex is natural. But self-control is a fruit of God's Spirit and keeping four feet on the floor is one practical way to practice self-control.

> **It really helps to keep blouses buttoned, pants zipped and erotic body parts covered.**

Rule 2: No clothes off!

It really helps to keep blouses buttoned, pants zipped and erotic body parts covered. Along with this rule is a good idea to not slip your hands under each other's clothing.

Rule 3: No erotic fondling!

Some places on our bodies tend to be more easily stimulated than others. These places certainly include the genitals, but breasts, necks, thighs, and earlobes are also top contenders for places to avoid in fingertip and kissing exploration. Some people also have other sensitive areas that need to be off-limits for them. How do you handle these individual idiosyncrasies? You speak the truth in love. "I don't know why touching my elbow like that does what it does to me, but it does, so don't".

Rule 4: No French kissing!

The tongue is definitely an erotic organ. Couples in courtship need to keep their own tongues behind their own teeth. No French kissing. It's an act of penetration. It is generally very effective in physically preparing the body for genital intercourse.

CHAPTER FOURTEEN

HARNESSING THE SEX DESIRE AND ENERGY

THE ISSUE OF PURITY IN pre-marital relationships needs to be given more attention than it is getting at the moment from churches and other Christian youth groups. Many young people relate with the opposite sex solely to satisfy their sexual desires. The unfortunate consequence has been broken hearts and relationships, unwanted pregnancies and ruined lives. All these consequences have still not made us take this issue seriously. It is almost as if both the church and the larger society have come to accept fornication as a permissible way of conducting courtship. It is now common to see young

> **"Fleeing" is always a more effective way to guarantee purity in any relationship...than putting yourself in tempting situations...**

people cohabiting as though they were married couples and no one dares to confront them about it.

My emphasis in the previous chapters has been more on avoiding the situation of stirring up sexual passion in yourself or your relationship partner by your actions in the relationship. That is in line with the scriptural injunction *to 'flee also youthful lust;...'* (2 Tim. 2:22). It is a known fact that: prevention is always better than cure. So "fleeing" is always a more effective way to guarantee purity in any relationship with the opposite sex than putting yourself in tempting situations that require striving to overcome such temptations.

Now and then, you will feel sexually aroused and your body will crave to get intimate with the opposite sex. It is usually worse for the males, who very often tend to experience early morning erections or erections from being exposed to erotic body parts of ladies as they move around. I know that ladies too, have occasions when they feel sexually aroused and desire to get intimate with the opposite sex. The honest question is: how can you handle the sexual arousal that you feel in a way that will not lead you to sin?

One way is through a process called sex transmutation. This process is a relevant concept and a necessary follow-up to the suggestions made in earlier chapters. Before I expound on it, I will love to point out that, feeling sexually aroused is natural and not sinful in itself. It is proof that your body is working the way God designed it to function. Thus the sexual urge you feel should never be confused with a prompt to indulge in fornication.

Sex Transmutation

It has been said that the emotion of sex brings into being a state of mind that many people generally associate with the physical. This is because of improper influences to which they have been subjected in their quest for knowledge about sex. Unfortunately, many things that are essentially physical have highly biased their minds. The bulk of this improper influence comes from junk information about sex from the print and electronic media as well as from cultural orientation.

Sex transmutation is a concept that encourages any human being to redirect their sexual emotions into something beneficial whenever it comes

Feeling sexually aroused is natural and not sinful in itself. It is proof that your body is working the way God designed it to function.

surging. It involves the switching of the mind, (when sexually aroused), from thoughts of physical expression of the sex urge to thoughts of some other none physical nature mostly of creative nature. I pointed out in one of the previous chapters that the sex desire is the most powerful human emotion and that it was God's idea. God in His infinite wisdom made this emotion a source of blessing to man if properly understood and harnessed. It is said that when experiencing this sexual desire, humans develop a keenness of imagination, courage, willpower, persistence and creative ability unknown to them at other times. This is why it is possible and necessary to make this mental switch so that this keenness of imagination and creative ability can be harnessed. When this switching is done, the motivating force maintains all its attributes mentioned above which can be used as powerful forces to create, invent, write, sing and express one's self creatively.

> **Sex transmutation is a concept that encourages any human being to redirect their sexual emotions into something beneficial whenever it comes surging.**

The transmutation of sex energy however requires a deliberate exercise of willpower. One must be deliberate about the choice to channel the energy that is generated during times of sexual arousal to the non-physical expressions as listed above. I believe that when you make it a practice to always pick up a pen and paper when you feel sexually aroused to think and write or compose something creative, you will be amazed at the

> **The transmutation of sex energy however requires a deliberate exercise of willpower.**

results you will get. Note that, it will take consistency to be able to achieve this mental switch.

Here is a paraphrase of what John Maxwell Taylor says on this topic: During times of sexual arousal, you need to be precisely aware that you are uniting sex-creative force with the higher centres of intelligence in the mental and emotional brains. This means engaging in an interiorizing of consciousness while sexually aroused. At this point you need to "focus upon not the physical pleasurable sensation you are feeling, but the subtle inner flows of sex energy that is being raised vibrationally to the same frequency as the soul.

Self Control

Sex transmutation cannot be achieved without self-control, so let me remind you of the importance of self-control in the life of a child of God. Every child of God who is indwelt by the Holy Spirit has the Spirit's enablement to be able to control his/her appetites and be able to stand

> **Every child of God who is indwelt by the Holy Spirit has the Spirit's enablement to be able to control his/her appetites and be able to stand tall through any tempting situations.**

tall through any tempting situations. It was my Dad who first pointed 1Cor. 10:13 to me and I have found it very helpful ever since. It is a verse that should give every Christian confidence in facing whatever temptations that come his/her way. It says: *"The only temptation that you have are the same temptations that all people have. But you can trust God. He will not let you be tempted more than you can bear. But when you are tempted, God will also give you a way to escape that temptation. Then you will be able to endure it"* (1 Cor. 10:13- ERB). God allows you to experience sexual arousal even as an unmarried person, because He knows you have the capacity to transmute that energy into something creative. Thus you have no excuse when you fail to do that but rather indulge in sexual sin.

Self-control is self-restraint and self-mastery- a mastery of your impulses and emotions. It is only when you have mastery of something that you will be able to channel and redirect it to something else. So it is with your sexual energy, your ability to harness it lies in first mastering and containing it, and can only be achieved through the exercise of the power of self-control which the Holy Spirit gives to as many as are willing to receive it.

Our sex energies hold great potential for helping us achieve tremendous creative results if we understand it and decide to give a shot at sex transmutation. However, for anyone who will not accept the concept of sex transmutation as a practical or attainable step further from self-control, then I will urge you to take the practice of self-control very seriously especially as it relates to your sexuality.

Let self-control be your working tool in ensuring that you hold back the physical expression of your sexuality until when you marry. God designed sex to be enjoyed only in the confines of marriage with your spouse; so any sex that you engage in before you are married will bring a curse upon you and your future in ways that you might not see immediately. So don't let the sex energy that surges within you be an excuse for indulging in fornication and other acts that displease our Lord and Master Jesus Christ.

Let self-control be your working tool in ensuring that you hold back the physical expression of your sexuality until when you marry.

CHAPTER FIFTEEN

CONLUSION

EVERYONE THAT DESIRES TO MARRY according to God's will nurtures a very noble desire and will have God's help in actualizing it. There is no doubting the fact that marriage was God's idea and He upholds as many as seek to enter into it honourably. God did not just think up marriage and leave it to us (his creatures) to figure it out by our instincts and wisdom. He laid down the principles guiding how to start a marriage and also how to make it work to fulfil His intended purpose. Therefore, your only guarantee for success in marriage is when you follow God's pattern for starting and running it.

My earnest desire for writing this book is to help you have a basic knowledge of how to start a relationship

> **Your only guarantee for success in marriage is when you follow God's pattern for starting and running it.**

and nurture it into a God honouring marriage. Marriage is romantic and the relationship that culminates into it is also inevitably romantic. How one walks the tightrope of enjoying the romance and at the same time avoiding sin can tell whether or not the relationship will end in a God honouring marriage. How a relationship begins and the character of the individuals involved in it are key indicators of its success or otherwise.

Marriage as God designed it is something so beautiful and powerful. It has great potential for affecting the lives of those in it, those around them and society as a whole. This is why the devil has chosen to fight marriages with his best weapons and with unwavering consistency. He begins the attack on the relationship. Once it is built on a faulty foundation and nurtured with bad character, it will certainly end up in a bitter marriage; which is the experience of many. If you go by what you see or hear about marriages, you might be tempted to think of it as a worthless thing. But nothing can be further from the truth. The problems you see and hear about in marriages can be attributed to one of two things:

1. The relationship was built on a wrong foundation, implying that, the marriage actually failed before it started. Same as the foolish builder Jesus told us about in Matthew 7:24 – 27.

2. The couple has refused to follow God's pattern for running the marriage and has refused to employ God's wisdom and skill in making their marriage as fulfilling as God intended it to be.

When you become born again, God fills you with His Spirit. As God's child, you have the Spirit of excellence in you, and that excellence Spirit should be seen in all aspects of your living, including the relationship

> **God's will is that you should show His praise and glory in your marriage for all to see and glorify His name.**

that leads to marriage. God's will is that you should show His praise and glory in your marriage for all to see and glorify His name, right from its formative years. This is achievable if you set it as your singular goal right from the beginning. Seeking to honour God in this aspect of your life will certainly get you God's backing and you can be sure that you will succeed.

REFERENCES

Robbie Castleman: True Love: in a world of false hope. Sex, Romance and Real People

Dean Sherman: Love, Sex and Relationships. YWAM Publishing, 1999.

Premarriage Counselling Manual: Challenge Marriage and Family Ministries

Nicky Gumbel: Questions of Life, A Practical Introduction to the Christian Faith. Cook communications ministries, North America. 1993, 1996.

Witness Lee: Character, Living Stream Ministry 1987, USA, distributed in Nigeria by: Precious Connections Ltd Lagos.

Goodrick & Kohlenberger : The NIV Exhaustive Concordance, Zondervan Publishing House, Grand Rapids, Michigan, 1999

Joshua Harris: boy meets girl say hello to courtship. Multnomah Books, 2000, 2005

Dale Carnegie: How to win friends and influence People; Pocket Books, 1998

www.ingramcontent.com/pod-product-compliance
Lightning Source LLC
Chambersburg PA
CBHW031334160726
47993CB00002B/675